J 582.13 REN
Rene, Ellen
Investigating how flowers
grow

112508

SCIENCE DETECTIVES

Investigating
How Flowers Grow

Ellen René

PowerKiDS

To my mother, who always sees beauty in the world

Published in 2009 by The Rosen Publishing Group, Inc.
29 East 21st Street, New York, NY 10010

First Edition

Editor: Joanne Randolph
Book Design: Julio Gil
Photo Researcher: Jessica Gerweck

Photo Credits: Cover, back cover (top center, top right, middle left, bottom left), pp. 5, 6, 9, 10, 13, 14, 17, 18 Shutterstock.com; back cover (middle center) © Jim Merli; back cover (middle right) © Fat Chance Productions; p. 21 © age fotostock/SuperStock.

Library of Congress Cataloging-in-Publication Data

René, Ellen.
  Investigating how flowers grow / Ellen Rene. — 1st ed.
      p. cm. — (Science detectives)
  Includes index.
  ISBN 978-1-4042-4484-9 (library binding)
  1. Flowers—Juvenile literature. 2. Plants—Development—Juvenile literature. I. Title.
  QK653.R43 2009
  582.13—dc22
                                          2008002338

Manufactured in the United States of America

Contents

Big Discovery

In 1878, a scientist found a monster on a Pacific island. It was huge. He could not put his arms around it. It towered over him. He needed two men to carry it. They tied it to a pole and put the pole on their shoulders. The monster stank like rotting meat. The monster's name was titan arum. It was a flower!

There are tiny flowers, too. A dozen duckweed flowers can fit on the head of a pin. There are many, many kinds of flowers. They come in all sizes, shapes, and colors. All flowers do one job, though. Do you know what it is? Let's find out!

The titan arum flower can grow to be 10 feet (3 m) tall. The flower's smell is meant to bring meat-eating bugs to the plant.

Sometimes sepals look like petals. A daffodil's outer yellow "petals" are large, colorful sepals.

What Are the Parts of a Flower?

Even though flowers look different, most have the same parts. Flowers sit on top of stems. Stems carry water from roots and food from leaves. **Sepals** grow where the flower and stem meet. They look like a circle of leaves. Sepals cover buds to keep them safe. After flowers bloom, most sepals are hard to see. Some drop off.

Inside the sepals is a circle of **petals**, the showy parts of flowers. Most are white or brightly colored. Some have special bottoms that make nectar, or a sweet juice. Petals are not a flower's real working parts, though.

Have you seen the green tops on strawberries? These green tops are sepals that remained after flowers became fruits. Fruits form from the parts of flowers that hold the eggs. A ripe fruit holds the seeds of the plant.

A Peek Inside

Each kind of flowering plant makes its own special pollen. The tiny grains come in many different shapes and sizes. The grains may be round, square, star shaped, bumpy, or smooth.

Flowers help plants make new plants. Some plants have male and female flowers. Most have male and female parts in the same flower. The female **pistil** is in the center. It is rounded at the bottom and is long and thin at the top. Its rounded bottom contains egg cells. Its thin neck, or **style**, ends in a tip, called the **stigma**.

Male **stamens** form a ring around the pistil. The long, thin stamens are topped by sacs, called anthers. Anthers contain **pollen**, a yellowish dust made of thousands of tiny grains.

This close-up of a lily shows the style and the stamens. Do you see the rounded stigma in the center and the long anthers on each stamen?

These are flowers that were pollinated. The flowers have died, and the ovary with the seeds has grown into a round, red seedpod.

How Do Flowers Make Seeds?

A flower's job is to make seeds. To form seeds, pollen grains and egg cells from the same kind of plant must join, or come together. Each holds part of what is needed to make a new plant.

When pollen grains land on the right stigma, the grains start to grow. Each grain forms a tube that moves down the style to the egg cells. When the tube reaches an egg cell, they join. This is called pollination, which helps the plant make seeds. Seeds hold tiny new plants and food to help them grow.

Not all flowering plants start out the same way. Most start from seeds. Some, like tulips, onions, and lilies, may also start as bulbs. Bulbs are like large underground buds that grow into new flowers. They store food and water for the growing plant.

A Food Factory?

Plants need food to grow, flower, and make seeds. Where do they get food, though? Their leaves change water and carbon dioxide, a gas in the air, into sugars for food. This is called **photosynthesis**. Photosynthesis needs sunlight and **chlorophyll** to work. Chlorophyll helps plants use sunlight to make food. It also makes plants look green.

How do plants sense when it is time to flower? For a long time, scientists thought plants needed the right amount of daylight to flower. Then, they discovered that plants really need the right amount of darkness to flower. Some need more. Some need less. Some are not that picky.

Sunlight

Oxygen

Carbon Dioxide

Water

This photo shows how photosynthesis works. The plant takes in water from its roots and carbon dioxide and light through its leaves.

13

This plant is just starting to grow. You can see the tops of the roots that it uses to take food and water from the soil.

Water and Soil

Like all living things, plants need water. Their roots take up water from the soil. This water contains **minerals** that get picked up from the soil. Plants need water and minerals to make important **chemicals** like chlorophyll. Water helps plants stay cool when it evaporates, or is given off by leaves as a gas. It also keeps plants firm. If they do not get enough water, they turn brown and die.

Soils are not all the same. They hold different amounts of air, water, and minerals. That is one reason plants may grow well in one place but not in another.

What Else Do Flowers Need?

What if plants have everything they need to grow? That means they have plenty of sun, air, water, and soil. Will their flowers make seeds? Not always. Why? What else do they need? Most need helpers to carry pollen from one flower to another. Often **insects** do the job.

Pollen sticks to insects as they go from bloom to bloom in search of food. Along the way, some pollen rubs off. If it lands on a stigma in the right kind of flower, pollination takes place. Some plants pollinate themselves. Others, like trees and grasses, use wind to spread their pollen around.

This bee is helping this flower pollinate. You can see the tiny yellow bits of pollen all over this bee's legs and body.

This plant uses its showy purple flowers to bring a butterfly to visit. The butterfly will spread pollen as it moves from flower to flower.

Come and Get It!

How do flowers get insects to come for a visit? They attract, or draw, them the same way cookie stores in the mall attract you. They use color, scent, and the promise of food. Insects do not see colors the same way people do. Many insects are attracted to flowers by colors we cannot see. Some flowers have markings that show insects where to land.

Mainly, insects come to flowers for nectar. A flower's bright colors and strong scent let them know where to find the nectar. They catch an insect's attention from far away. Some plants do not make nectar. They attract insects that eat pollen.

Who Are the Pollinators?

Do you know why farmers do their best to keep orchards free of weeds? Farmers do not want bees to visit bright yellow dandelions instead of fruit trees.

There are many different insects that do the important job of pollinating flowers. Some birds and bats help spread pollen, too.

Bees visit showy, bright flowers to feed on nectar and pollen. They are important pollinators of flowering fruit trees, such as apple and cherry trees.

Butterflies fly from flower to flower during the day. They put their long tongues inside the flowers to sip nectar. They carry bits of pollen from the other plants they have visited. Moths are busy at night. White or pale flowers attract them.

This moth feeds on a sweet-smelling flower. Flowers pollinated by moths send out strong scents to help the moths find them.

Flower Power

Flowers add beauty to our world. We enjoy their colors and scents. Their seeds grow into plants we use for food, housing, and clothing. Some flowers are good to eat. Broccoli and cauliflower are both flowers.

Scientists can spend a lifetime investigating just one kind of flower. By studying plants and flowers, scientists have found many important medicines, or things that can help us feel better when we are sick. Are you good at watching the world around you? Look at a garden. What do you see? Take notes. Draw pictures. Maybe someday you will make a big discovery, too.

Glossary

chemicals (KEH-mih-kulz) Matter that can be mixed with other matter to cause changes.

chlorophyll (KLOR-uh-fil) Green matter inside plants that allows them to use energy from sunlight to make their own food.

insects (IN-sekts) Small animals that often have six legs and wings.

minerals (MIN-rulz) Natural things that are not animals, plants, or other living things.

petals (PEH-tulz) Colorful parts of a flower.

photosynthesis (foh-toh-SIN-thuh-sus) The way in which green plants make their own food from sunlight, water, and a gas called carbon dioxide.

pistil (PIS-tuhl) The female part of the flower.

pollen (PAH-lin) A yellow dust made by the male parts of flowers.

sepals (SEE-pulz) Parts that look like little green leaves that cover the outside of a flower bud to keep the flower safe before it opens.

stamens (STAY-munz) Male parts of flowers. The stamen carries the pollen.

stigma (STIG-muh) The sticky bump on a flower that catches pollen.

style (STYL) A long, tubelike part of a flower that carries pollen to the ovary, or place where the egg cells are.

Index

C
chlorophyll, 12, 15
color(s), 4, 19, 22

I
insects, 7, 16, 19–20
island, 4

K
kind(s), 4, 22

M
meat, 4

minerals, 15
monster, 4

N
name, 4

P
petals, 7
photosynthesis, 12
pin, 4
pistil, 8
pole, 4
pollen, 8, 16, 19–20

S
scientist(s), 4, 12, 22
sepals, 7
shapes, 4
shoulders, 4
sizes, 4
stamens, 8
stems, 7
stigma, 8, 11, 16
style, 8, 11

T
titan arum, 4

Web Sites

Due to the changing nature of Internet links, PowerKids Press has developed an online list of Web sites related to the subject of this book. This site is updated regularly. Please use this link to access the list:
www.powerkidslinks.com/scidet/flowers/